Facts About the Chinese Giant Salamander

By Lisa Strattin

© 2016 Lisa Strattin

Facts for Kids Picture Books by Lisa Strattin

Sign Up for New Release Emails Here

LisaStrattin.com/subscribe-here

Join the KidCrafts Monthly Program Here

KidCraftsByLisa.com

Contents

INTRODUCTION

The Chinese Giant Salamanders are highly endangered creatures, which means there are not many of them left in the world. This is because of pollution and loss of habitat. In addition, some people illegally trap them in the wild and then turn around and sell them to other people for money. Some of those people bring them to pet stores and they are sold to the public as pets. This is a sad situation that wildlife authorities are trying to stop. To counter the loss of this creature in the wild, there are breeding facilities now trying to increase their numbers.

CHARACTERISTICS

The Chinese Giant Salamander is harmless to humans. It has very poor eyesight, so it relies on vibrations caused by movements in the water to find its prey. They do have lungs for breathing air but these don't work very well. Adults actually breathe through their skin. Frogs can do this too. Some types of salamanders can spend equal time in the water and out of the water, but this particular species must stay in the water at all times or their skin will dry out. They are nocturnal which means they sleep during the day and are active at night.

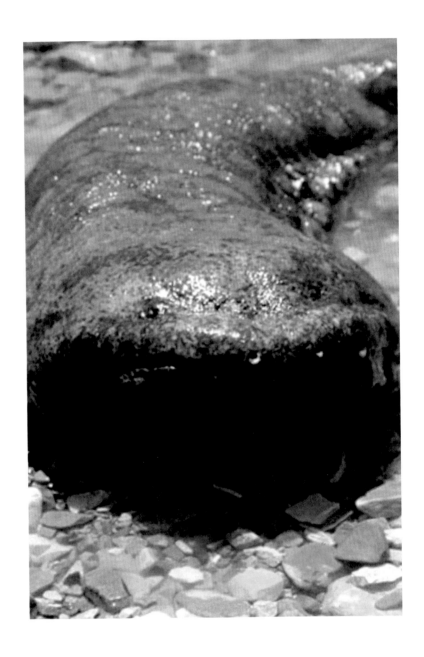

APPEARANCE

The most obvious feature of this animal is its size – it is huge. Most salamanders are small enough to fit in your hand. This one is bigger than you are. You will also notice the big and flat triangular-shaped head and jaws, four short legs, feet, and a long fat tail. They have small eyes and no eyelids. They are brown in color with patches of black and dark green to blend into its environment. Their skin is wrinkly.

LIFE STAGES

Life begins as an egg. The female can lay hundreds of eggs in the water at one time. The next stage is larvae. The baby breaks out of its egg and swims using its tail. It does not yet have legs. They look similar to tadpoles which develop into frogs. The salamander develops legs and continues to grow larger into adulthood.

LIFE SPAN

Scientists estimate that these animals can live as long as 50 to 80 years.

SIZE

Adults measure between 5 to 6 feet long. They are the largest amphibian in the world.

HABITAT

They are found in the mountain forest regions of China where they live in cold running streams and shallow lakes.

DIET

All salamanders are carnivores – they eat other animals. Their diet includes fish, frogs, worms, crayfish, crabs, and bugs.

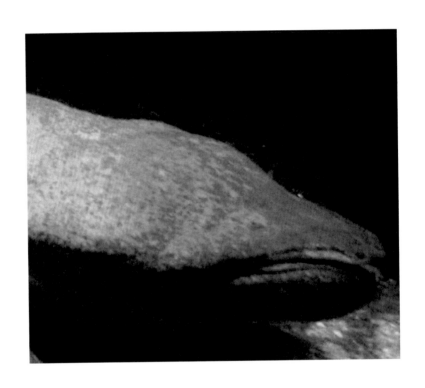

FRIENDS AND ENEMIES

It is unknown if the Chinese Giant Salamander has any friends, but humans are their main enemies. People have hunted them to near-extinction.

SUITABILITY AS PETS

This animal does not make a suitable pet. It is against the law to buy and keep one in your home. Even if you could buy one, think about the size and weight of this salamander. They are bigger and weigh more than you. It would be difficult to pick one up and carry it around. You cannot train it to walk with you on a leash. They have a powerful bite and could hurt you. Your family would need to build a big enclosure with rocks and streams of cold running water which would be very expensive.

There are so few of these giants left. If you want to have a salamander as a pet, there are smaller breeds that are suitable. The best idea is to visit a pet store that specializes in reptiles and amphibians, have a look around, ask many questions, and learn as much as you can before you make your choice for a pet.

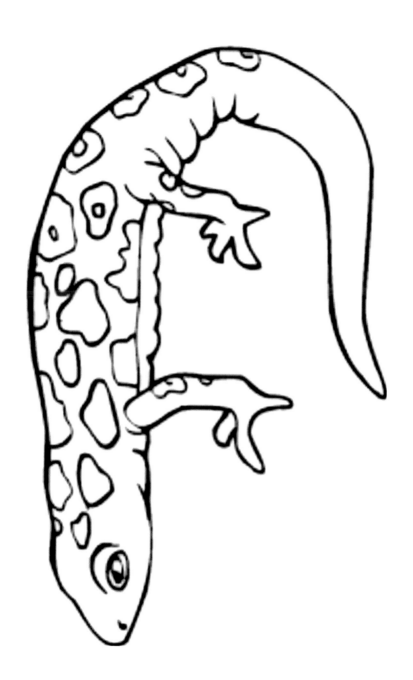

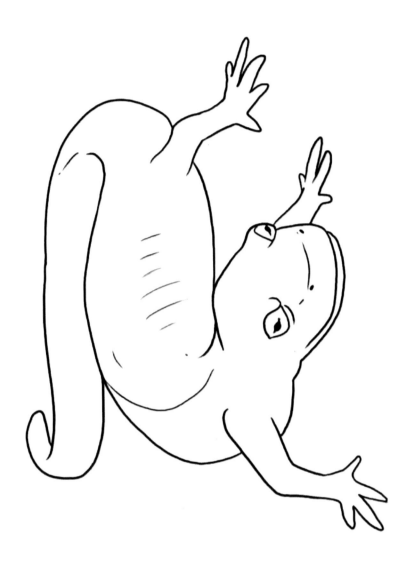

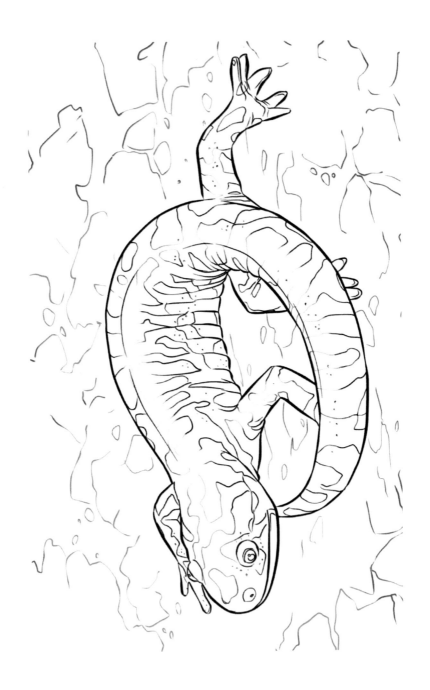

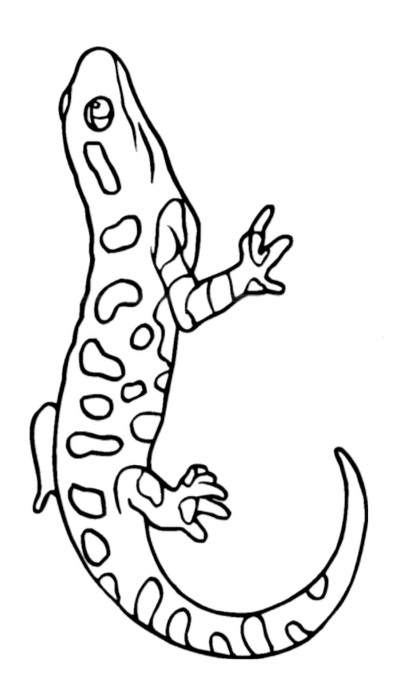

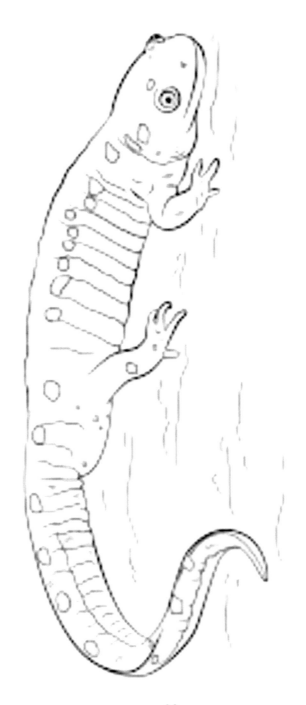

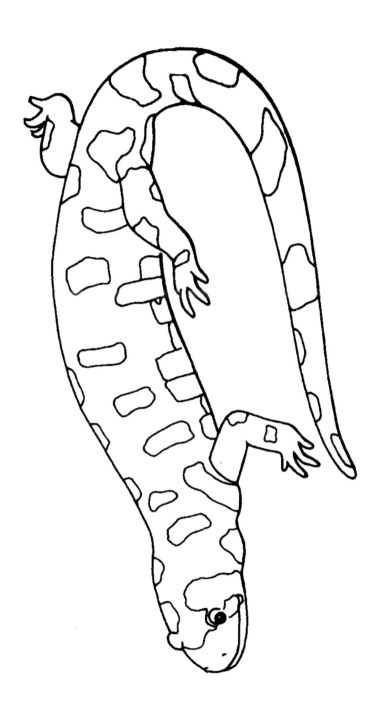

Please leave me a review here:

http://lisastrattin.com/Review-Vol-90

For more Kindle Downloads Visit Lisa Strattin Author Page on Amazon Author Central

http://amazon.com/author/lisastrattin

To see upcoming titles, visit my website at LisaStrattin.com– all books available on kindle!

http://lisastrattin.com

PLUSH SALAMANDER TOY

You can get one by copying and pasting this link into your browser: **http://lisastrattin.com/SalamanderToy**

KIDCRAFTS MONTHLY SUBSCRIPTION PROGRAM

Receive a Kids Craft and a Lisa Strattin Full Color Paperback Book Each Month in Your Mailbox!

Get yours by copying and pasting this link into your browser

KidCraftsByLisa.com

Made in the USA
Lexington, KY
14 February 2018